LILLENAS®
DRAMA

EASTER PROGRAM BUILDER no. 30

Creative Resources for Program Directors

Compiled by Kim Messer

lillenas
PUBLISHING COMPANY
a division of nazarene publishing house

PO Box 419527
Kansas City, MO 64141

Questions? Please write or call:
Lillenas Publishing Company
Drama Resources
P.O. Box 419527
Kansas City, MO 64141
Phone: 816-931-1900 • Fax: 816-412-8390
E-mail: drama@lillenas.com
Web Site: www.lillenasdrama.com

Cover Design: J.R. Caines

CONTENTS

Recitations for Preschool

Up from the Grave

Up from the grave,
Jesus to save,
Now we can say,
Happy Easter Day!

K. R. Messer

This Little Kid

Thank You, Jesus, for what You did
You rose and saved this little kid.

Ray Ressem

Eternal King

Hurry, come see,
The morning breaks,
All creation sings.

Christ is risen
From the grave,
Our Redeemer, Lord,
And King.

Robert Colbert

Hurray!

Hurray! Hurray!
It's Easter Day.
Welcome to our happy play!

K. R. Messer

Time to Cheer

It's really here,
A time to cheer.
Jesus is alive!

Karen Lee

Easter Day Is Great!

Come, come
Play today!
Help us celebrate!

Come, come
Shout hurray
Easter Day is great!

Ray Ressem

Our Jesus Is Great

It's beautiful out!
Don't fret; don't pout.
Let's celebrate!
Our Jesus is great.

K. R. Messer

All Because

CHILD 1: Hallelujah!
CHILD 2: Praise be to God!
CHILD 3: Easter time is real,
CHILD 4: And it's all because . . .
ALL: Jesus lives!

Robert Colbert

Jesus Is Here

Jesus is here,
Oh happy day!
Jesus rose on
Easter Day!

K. R. Messer

The Easter Egg

The Easter Egg
Means new life.
Jesus risen
Means new life.
Alleluia!

Karen Lee

Be Glad

Be glad; be happy
Hip and hooray
Jesus Christ is risen today!

K. R. Messer

Happy Resurrection

Christ is risen,
The victory is won.
Happy resurrection
To everyone!

Robert Colbert

Easter Is Great

Easter is great,
Easter is good,
Pretty flowers,
Yummy food.

But best of all
I have to say,
Jesus is alive today!

K. R. Messer

Recitations for Ages 5 to 7

Awesome

What you did is awesome.
You really showed you cared.
The road, the cross, the grave,
You went where no one dared.

Ray Ressem

Christ Is Risen

The cross is bare,
The tomb is empty.
Grave where is
Your stain?
For Christ is risen,
He reigns on high.
All glory to His name.

Robert Colbert

Thank You

Thank You, Jesus, for today!
Thank You, Jesus, that You save.
Thank You for the way You died.
Thank You for the sacrifice.

K. R. Messer

His Greatest Gift

The cross is empty,
What a blessed sight.
Jesus died for you and me.
To share eternal light.

He gives us peace,
He gives us love.
But His greatest gift
Is shared life above.

Karen Lee

Easter! Easter!

Easter! Easter!
You came today.
Easter! Easter!
Don't go away.
We feel happy, sunny, and fun
All because of God's Son

Jesus! Jesus!
You rose today.
Jesus! Jesus!
Hurray, hurray.
We feel happy, sunny, and fun.
Jesus is the only One.

Thank you! Thank you!
We love today.
Thank you! Thank you!
We have to say
We feel happy, sunny, and fun
Because of what the Savior's done!

K. R. Messer

You Ready?

(Use signs to prompt the audience and add movements to enhance this "cheer." Also can be followed by an energetic song.)

We want to hear you say it.
Yes, Jesus came to save.

We want for you to shout your praise.
Get ready, shout, "hurray!"

(Child holds up sign that reads "HURRAY!")

You ready? Shout, "hurray!"

(Child holds up sign that reads "HURRAY!")

We love to hear you say it.
Yes, Jesus rose today.

We want for you to shout your praise.
Get ready, shout, "hurray!"

(Child holds up sign that reads "HURRAY!")

You ready? Shout, "hurray!"

(Child holds up sign that reads "HURRAY!")

Yeah!

(Kids shout and cheer as they exit stage.)

Ray Ressem

Pretty Girl

My mommy says that I look pretty
In my new hat and dress.
I'm not allowed to play much, though,
In case I make a mess.

K. R. Messer

Easter Food

My jacket is like Daddy's.
I think that I look good.
But what I really want is
A taste of Easter food.

K. R. Messer

Recitations for Ages 8 to 10

It's Hard for Me to Imagine

(This reading can be done by one or more students.)

Sometimes it's hard for me to
imagine Jesus dying on a cross.
It's not easy to stop and think about
how God suffered His loss.
Most of the time all I think about is
what's going on in my day.
But on Easter, I don't want to forget
the price He had to pay.

Ray Ressem

I'm Thankful for Easter

Easter toys and baskets
Seem to go together
Like daffodils and tulips
Go with springtime weather.

But Easter wouldn't be Easter
Without the wonderful story
Of the Savior who came to earth
And left His home in glory.

I'm glad that Jesus loved us
Enough that He chose to die
So that we can live with Him
Forever in the sky.

Margaret Primrose

Jesus Died to Save the World

We're sorry that you have to go,
But before you leave you need to
know
That what you heard and saw today
Won't ever, ever go away.

Jesus died to save the world.
He came for every boy and girl.
Now if you're thinking, "Not for
me!"
Remember what this day you've
seen:

A God who gave His precious
Treasure;
A Savior's love that has no measure;
They gave to save us—you and me,
They gave so that we could be free.

So go your way—smile on your face.
Remember that He took your place.
Believe with all your heart and
know
The Savior's love inside you grows.

K. R. Messer

Think About

Think about Peter who denied Him
three times.
Think of His friends who ran from
His side.
Think of the women, His mother
there crying.
Think of the crowd standing;
watching Him dying.

Think about morning; the bright
shining sun.
Think of the promise being fulfilled
and done.
Think of how Jesus came out of the
grave.
Think about how He did it to save.

Ray Ressem

Paid for All Our Sins

We're lucky and blessed to have
what we do,
A Savior that loves beyond
measure.

We have an amazing Father above
Preparing our heavenly treasure.

But what we have to decide on our
own
Is what we will do with Jesus.

The Son who paid for all our sins
Daily and humbly seeks us.

Ray Ressem

His Plans for Us

When Jesus prayed in the garden
Of dark Gethsemane,
He didn't just pray for himself;
He prayed for you and me.

He knew that He would die
For a world of sinful men.
He also knew He would rise,
Never to die again.

He proved that He was alive
After He rose from the grave.
"Go and make disciples"
Was the last command He gave.

He disappeared in a cloud
But will come again some day.
I'm glad I've trusted Jesus
To take my sins away.

He's preparing mansions for us—
For all of you, and me—
I'm glad our invitation
Is for all eternity.

Margaret Primrose

Plays & Monologues for All Ages

WERE YOU THERE

A Monologue for Communion or Good Friday

by John Cashion

Themes: Crucifixion, Good Friday

Synopsis: Peter, the disciple, introducing the stanzas of the spiritual, "Were You There?"

Cast:

PETER

Production Notes: You may have a solo voice or ensemble singing the verses of the song as indicated.

PETER: "Were you there when they crucified my Lord?"

I was—at least I was close by. Before everything unraveled I was so brave, so sure of myself. Then at the moment when He most needed a friend . . . I pretended not to know Him.

The crowing of a rooster was for me a pronouncement of judgment. Sometimes . . . it causes me to tremble, in fear and shame.

I was there when they crucified my Lord.

(Stanza one sung)

"Were you there when they nailed Him to a tree?"

I was there—but I wasn't close enough to see. I could not have watched anyway. But I heard those blows of an angry Roman hammer—and they echoed in my empty, aching heart.

My shame grew with each impact, with each metallic thud. Again I trembled . . . weeping and sorrowful.

I was there when they nailed Him to a tree.

(Stanza two sung)

"Where you there when they laid Him in the tomb?"

I was there—watching from a distance, as usual. One of the rulers brought Him to a tomb. The women planned to prepare Him for burial, but not yet, for the Sabbath had come.

It was over, yet still I trembled. Yet, the certainty of my loss was tempered by a tantalizing possibility.

He had spoken of resurrection, of victory, of joy. Those words were but a faint memory now, but a memory that refused to die. Perhaps there was another chance for me. Perhaps there is for you.

Were you there when they laid Him in the tomb?

(Stanza three sung. Depending upon nature of service, monologue could end here or continue with final verse.)

"Were you there when He rose up from the grave?"

I was not there—none of us were when it actually happened. The evidence was compelling, but who could believe it?

And then, I heard His voice . . . I felt His presence . . . I saw His hands. That tantalizing possibility had become an amazing reality. And again I trembled . . . with joy and excitement.

The women said He called my name—singled me out, as He so often had before. When I heard that, I knew He had not abandoned me, although I had deserted Him.

And He has not . . . will not . . . abandon you, no matter what you have done.

Were you there when He rose up from the grave?

(Stanza four sung)

NEAR THE CROSS

A Service for Lent That Includes Communion

by Rebecca Thompson

This service works well in a dimly lit sanctuary with a well-lit cross. The scriptural readings and the narration should flow together seamlessly. After Communion, the sanctuary lights can be extinguished, leaving only the cross lit.

The songs included are simply suggestions; there are many other songs that would be equally appropriate.

Instrumental Prelude: *Near the Cross*, by Fanny J. Crosby and William H. Doane, © 1869

Welcome

Congregational Choruses

Above All, by Lenny LeBlanc and Paul Baloche (Integrity's Hosanna! Music, © 1999)

Once Again, by Matt Redman (Kingsway's Thankyou Music, © 1995)

NARRATOR: There were many at the cross that day: soldiers . . . priests . . . criminals . . . faithful women . . . passive observers . . . angry men. Tonight we're going to imagine that we are there among them. Let's see what they saw. Let's picture how *we* might have felt. There are no props here and no costumes. This is not a play, but a drama is about to unfold nevertheless. The cross stands center stage. All eyes are on Jesus.

The story is familiar. Jesus has been accused and tried and sentenced to die . . .

READER 1: Mark 15:16-20

NARRATOR: The soldiers are easy to dislike, aren't they? It wasn't enough to lead Jesus to His death. They stripped Him. They spit on Him. They attempted to humiliate Him. They beat Him. They mocked Him. Why? What had Jesus ever done to harm them? Some might argue that they were just doing their job, but did the "job" require them to laugh at Him? Was there some rule that said they must strike Him "again and again"?

As the Son of God, Jesus could have called down fire and brimstone. As a mere man, He could have fought back or at least defended himself. But as the One who is both fully God and fully man, He did the unthinkable. He forgave them.

READER 2: Mark 15:21-23; Luke 23:32-34*a*

Congregational: *Blessed Redeemer* (vs. 1-2), by Avis B. Christiansen and Harry Dixon Loes (Singspiration Music, © 1921)

NARRATOR: There were others there with Jesus, dying that day . . . common criminals who deserved this punishment for their deeds. Northing extraordinary here—just ordinary men who had lived less than perfect lives and were now faced with the consequences of their choices. There was nothing unique about *them*. It was the grace that Jesus offered that was truly astonishing.

READER 3: Luke 23:35-43

NARRATOR: Now you are probably not a criminal, but maybe you've lived your life as a "commoner" instead of as a child of the King. Maybe your past is full of decisions that haunt you or actions that cannot be undone. Maybe your choices have too often led you away from your Creator.

The criminal was there that day to give us hope. He had done nothing to deserve forgiveness. He had no time left to make amends. But there is good news in this repentant thief. It is not too late! You decide where you will spend eternity. You can choose to walk unashamed in the way of the world; or you can turn in repentance to the One who created you to live with Him. Call on His name. Fall on your knees. Ask Him to remember you. Your sin is not too great. Your repentance has not come too late. Seek Him. After all, you are the reason that He came.

Solo: *By the Way of the Cross* (vs. 1-2), by Dennis Wilson (Gaither Music Company, © 1995)

READER 4: John 19:25-27

NARRATOR: As He hung on the cross that day, in agony, soon to be separated from His heavenly Father for the first time in all eternity, you might think that He would be unaware of those around Him. Intent upon completing His mission on earth, it would be understandable if He simply tuned out all but that. But He didn't. Instead we see a good son, concerned about leaving behind His beloved mother. Not only was He aware of her, but as He was dying, He thought about how difficult it might be for her once He was gone. He thought about how alone she might feel. He worried about who would provide for her. Does this seem inconsequential to you? It is, of course, overshadowed by the other events of that day, but it has so much meaning. This is a Savior who cares about the detail of our lives. In the middle of the biggest spiritual battle ever to be fought, He thought about an earthly woman and her physical needs. Jesus wants to redeem us from our sin and reconcile us to the Father. But He also desires to provide for us day by day—food, shelter, companionship, protection. You can turn to Him with any request. He has already proven that He cares. You can trust Him with the details.

Congregation: *Cares Chorus*, by Kelly Willard (Maranatha Music, © 1978 & 1986)

NARRATOR: The scene was not peaceful that day. No, it was an awful day. An ugly day. There was nothing beautiful about this sacrifice. Like all sacrifices offered for the atonement of sin, blood was required, and it flowed freely from Jesus' head and hands and feet. It was painful just to look at Him. The torn flesh. The pierced hands, no longer healing. The perfect voice, no longer teaching, but crying out in abandonment.

And yet, there was something very beautiful inside this man. Can you see the love that must have brought Him to this place? Do you see the compassion in His eyes? Look closely. Under the battered and bruised body beats the heart of God's spotless, unblemished Lamb.

Solo: *Watch the Lamb*, by Ray Boltz (Shepherd Boy Music, © 1986)

Communion

Music: *How Beautiful*, by Twila Paris (Mountain Spring Music, © 1990)

NARRATOR: So there He was. Beaten, bleeding, dying. Betrayed by Judas. Denied by Peter. Left alone by His disciples. Surrounded by strangers. Abandoned by the Father.

Where would you have been? Weeping with Mary? Hiding with the disciples? Hurling insults at an innocent man? Or waiting silently in the crowd to see what He would do? It's hard to say. We are a fickle people, swayed by emotion. But not Jesus. He is always the same . . . yesterday . . . that day . . . every day . . .

As usual, His eyes were focused on people. Not just humanity, but individuals . . . His mother . . . a criminal . . . John . . . That day at Calvary, I think He saw more than just the faces of those around Him. I think He saw the hearts of all those He loved and all those He would some day call His own.

You were there—on His mind that day. In His heart. And where are you today? Are you weeping for the One who bled for you? Are you lingering at the foot of the Cross, wanting only to be near the One who gave all that He was, who sacrificed everything, just to draw near to you?

READER 5: Mark 15:33-39

Solo: *How Can I Say No*, by Mickey Cates (Straight Way Music, © 1981)

HOPE RENEWED

A Short Easter Play

by Beth Westcott

Synopsis: Jill's husband died a year ago, leaving her alone with two children. She is struggling as a single mom, financially and spiritually. Recently her mother also died, leaving her father (George) alone in his big house. It was decided that George would come to live with Jill, Josh, and Mandy. Josh isn't sure he wants Grandpa to live with them, but Mandy is willing to try. Mandy and Josh both miss their father. Jill is hoping that having Grandpa there will fill in some of the missing pieces for her struggling family.

Cast:

GEORGE—Senior adult male (Grandpa)
JILL—Adult female (Mom)
MANDY—Preteen or young teen girl, a little older than brother Josh
JOSH—Preteen or young teen boy

Setting: Spring, shortly before Easter; takes place in the back yard.

Production Notes: This play can be used as a regular stage drama or be done in readers theatre style. For readers theatre, the script may be read or memorized. If read, use expression and practice so that you don't sound like you are reading. Face the audience using microphones.

The cast should be in appropriate contemporary dress. Music may be added between scenes—choir, congregational, or specials.

Scene 1

(JILL, MANDY, *and* JOSH *enter the backyard.* JOSH *and* MANDY *carry backpacks, ready to leave for school.)*

JOSH *(whining)*: But Mom, why does Grandpa have to come here?

JILL: Grandpa is lonely. He doesn't like living in that big house all by himself.

MANDY: It doesn't seem the same without Grandma. I really miss her.

JILL: I do too, Mandy.

JOSH: Why can't Grandpa just get an apartment in the Senior Center?

JILL: He probably could, Josh, but we have plenty of room here. And besides, I'd like to know someone was here with you while I'm at work.

JOSH: I can take care of myself.

MANDY: You'd starve if you had to cook for yourself. Yuck—I remember the last time you fixed a meal.

JOSH: Just be quiet, Mandy!

JILL: OK, OK. Stop the fighting. I think . . . I think I'd feel better knowing you and Grandpa had each other.

MANDY *(brushing away a tear)*: I wish Daddy was still here.

JILL: Me too, dear.

(Pause while JILL *wipes her tears and* JOSH *folds his arms.)*

JILL: So, it's all right that we asked Grandpa to come?

JOSH: As long as I don't have to give up my room. Sean had to give up his room when his aunt came for a visit. He had to sleep in with his two little brothers.

MANDY: Josh, you know we fixed up the den for Grandpa. That way he doesn't have to climb the stairs.

JILL: You won't have to give up your room, Josh.

JOSH: Well, I guess it's OK.

JILL: I'm glad you agree, Josh, since Grandpa is coming today.

MANDY: Mom, after Grandpa comes, will we go back to church?

JILL *(shrugs)*: We'll see. Right now you kids need to get to school. I don't want you to be late.

*(*JILL *exits SR,* JOSH *and* MANDY *exit SL.)*

Scene 2

*(*JILL *and* GEORGE *enter;* GEORGE *is carrying a suitcase.)*

GEORGE: You know, Jill, I'm grateful that you and the kids invited me to live with you. It was a long winter.

JILL *(nodding)*: It's been hard for all of us. I'm glad you're here, Dad.

GEORGE: You've faced many changes in the last year. Ken was a good husband and father. *(sets down suitcase)*

JILL: Yes, yes, he was. I miss him terribly. It's hard being a single parent. *(big sigh)* Josh and Mandy are good kids, but they need a man's hand to steady them, especially Josh. Sometimes I don't know what to do.

GEORGE *(cheerfully)*: Well, today's Wednesday. I sure do look forward to the weekend, especially Sunday and church. There's nothing like worshiping with other believers. My Christian family helped me a lot after your mother died. Our friends help us through the bad times, don't you think?

JILL: I . . . well . . . I . . . we . . . we haven't been back to church since Ken died.

GEORGE *(surprised)*: Why is that, Jill?

JILL: I don't know. I was so angry at first, and I found it hard to go without Ken. Sunday morning became such a hassle, trying to get the kids ready and out on time. Then we became busy with other things, and I have to work . . .

GEORGE: I plan to go on Sunday, and I hope all of you will join me.

JILL *(shrugs)*: We'll see. Josh and Mandy should be home soon.

(Suddenly there's a scream from offstage. JOSH *enters SL and runs across stage yelling, "Help!"* MANDY *is close behind trying to grab him.)*

MANDY: I'm gonna get you, Josh! What did I do to deserve a brother like you?

*(*JILL *and* GEORGE *watch with opened mouths. Kids exit.)*

JILL: I think they're home. *(sigh)* I wonder what Josh did now? *(follows them out)*

GEORGE *(chuckling)*: Boys will be boys. *(carries suitcase off SR)*

Scene 3

*(*GEORGE *is raking the flower garden.* MANDY *enters.)*

MANDY: Hi, Grandpa. What are you doing?

GEORGE: Thinking about your grandma. She did love her flowers. *(pause)* There they are!

MANDY: What did you find, Grandpa? *(leaning over to see)*

GEORGE: Daffodils! I guess spring is here.

MANDY: Mom loves flowers too. She probably got that from Grandma. She doesn't get much time to spend in the flower garden now, since . . . since my dad died.

GEORGE *(leaning on rake)*: What do you remember best about your father?

MANDY *(smiling)*: Well, he worked hard and took care of us. He always had time for us. He came to our school programs, took us to church, played with us. And he loved Mom. *(sadly)* Now Mom doesn't even have the time to do anything but work.

GEORGE: I like to garden because it makes me feel closer to Grandma. How she loved to see things grow—her lilies, her grandchildren, all living things. Well, she didn't want to see me grow, she said, so she tried to be careful what she fed me. She is in heaven now, rejoicing in the presence of God, but I miss her.

(GEORGE resumes raking.)

MANDY: I'm glad you came to live with us, Grandpa. Maybe we won't be so lonely.

GEORGE: Say, what was it that your brother did that had you all fired up after school?

MANDY: Oh, little brothers can be such a pain. He's always trying to butt in on my friends and me. I wish he'd leave us alone and be quiet.

GEORGE: I'm glad to see he survived.

MANDY: Yeah, that's what moms do best—rescue pesky brothers.

(JOSH enters, hands in pockets.)

JOSH: Hi. What's going on here?

MANDY *(a little annoyed at the interruption)*: We're just talking.

JOSH: About what?

MANDY: About Grandma and flowers and . . . and Dad.

JOSH: Oh. *(There's a pause in the conversation while GEORGE rakes.)* Grandpa, I was wondering . . .

GEORGE *(straightening up)*: Yes, Josh?

JOSH: Well, I . . . There's a game after school tomorrow. It's our first game, and I was wondering . . . that is . . . *(pause)*

GEORGE: I love baseball. May I come to watch you play?

JOSH *(smiling)*: Sure, Grandpa. I was hoping you would come.

GEORGE. I'd be glad to. I know your mother works Thursday afternoons, so I'd be glad to go. How about you, Mandy?

MANDY: I'll go with you, Grandpa.

GEORGE: How about going to church with me on Sunday? I'd sure like company this week.

(MANDY *and* JOSH *look down and shuffle their feet.)*

JOSH: We don't have time for church anymore. Mom works all week and has to have Sunday to buy groceries and do things around the house.

MANDY: We haven't been to church for a long time. Mom keeps finding excuses.

GEORGE: I'll tell you what, if I do the grocery shopping and all of us help around the house, maybe your mother will find the time to go to church. What do you think?

JOSH: I guess it will be OK.

MANDY: Mom was mad at God and didn't want to go to church anymore.

JOSH: Sometimes it's hard to figure God out. I mean, my dad was a good person. He was even a Christian. And yet, that drunk driver hit him. Why did God let that happen?

GEORGE: We can't always understand why God allows what He allows. You'd go crazy trying to out-guess God. That's where faith comes in—believing that God is all-wise and wants what is best for us, even when everything seems wrong. Proverbs 3:5 and 6 says, "Trust in the LORD with all your heart, and lean not on your own understanding: In all your ways acknowledge him, and he shall direct your paths."

JOSH *(shaking his head):* I don't know, Grandpa. I just don't understand.

MANDY: I have to finish my homework. I have a paper due. *(moves toward exit)*

JOSH: I'm finished with my homework. Want to play a game of chess with me, Grandpa?

GEORGE: I guess I'm finished here for now. Where's the chessboard?

(They exit SR.)

Scene 4

*(*GEORGE, MANDY, *and* JOSH *enter SL.)*

GEORGE: That was a great game, Josh. How did you learn to hit the ball that way?

JOSH *(wearing baseball cap and carrying glove):* Dad taught me. We used to practice a lot.

GEORGE: I really enjoyed watching you play. Thanks for asking me. Well, let's get busy. We want to get supper made before your mother gets home.

MANDY: Mom will be so surprised. She's tired when she gets done with work.

JOSH: She never wanted us to do it, even though we volunteered.

MANDY: Maybe she thought we couldn't make our own meals, but I love to cook.

JOSH: I think she feels guilty if she doesn't do it.

GEORGE: You're probably right, Josh. Your mom is finding it hard to be a single parent. But I'm here to help now.

MANDY: Do you think our mom will ever get married again?

JOSH *(angrily)*: Mandy!

GEORGE *(chuckling)*: Do you have someone in mind, Mandy?

MANDY: Oh no, I just wondered. I have friends who have stepfathers.

GEORGE: How would you feel if your mother did marry again?

MANDY *(thoughtfully)*: I don't know. I suppose it would be OK if it's the right person.

JOSH: He'd have to be awfully good for me to agree.

GEORGE: If your mother finds a man who loves the Lord, loves her, and wants to take care of her, don't you think it would be all right?

JOSH: But she has you and us. Why would she have to get married again?

GEORGE: You know, Josh, I'm old. Who knows how long it will be before God calls me to heaven. And in just a few years, you and Mandy will have lives of your own.

JOSH: I suppose.

MANDY: Mom said maybe we'll all go to church with you on Sunday, if we get our work done.

GEORGE: Good. We'll have to be sure it's done.

(All exit SR.)

Scene 5

*(*MANDY *and* JOSH *enter SR.)*

MANDY: I don't know, Josh. Mom always finds excuses for not going.

JOSH: I know, but Grandpa's here now and . . .

MANDY: All of a sudden you seem to think it's great to have Grandpa around.

JOSH: Well, I had to get used to the idea. Now that he's here, it's not too bad.

(JILL *enters SL, home from work.)*

MANDY: Hi, Mom. How was your day?

JILL: Long and tiring. I'm sorry, I shouldn't complain.

JOSH: Maybe I'll get a job.

JILL: Not during the school year, Josh. Maybe this summer you can find something. By the way, how was your game?

JOSH: We won! I made a home run and brought in two other runners!

JILL: I'm proud of you, Josh. I just wish I could have been there for you.

MANDY: Mrs. Canner asked me to baby-sit tomorrow night. Will that be all right with you?

JILL: I don't think there's anything else on the schedule.

MANDY: May we go to church on Sunday? Mrs. Canner said there's a special service.

JOSH: Yeah, Mom, it's Easter. You said maybe we'd go.

JILL: Oh, I don't know. We have so much to do on Sunday.

MANDY: You always make excuses, Mom. If Dad were here, we would go.

JILL *(sharply)*: But he's not here.

JOSH: But Grandpa is, and Grandpa . . .

JILL: I know. I know. Grandpa wants us to go. But there's so much to do.

MANDY: What Josh was trying to tell you is, Grandpa volunteered to do the housework and grocery shopping so we can all go to church with him.

JOSH: And we're helping.

JILL: I . . . well . . . I don't know. I really hadn't planned . . .

MANDY: So let's do it anyway. All those years when you and Dad made us go, sometimes I wanted to stay home or do something else. But when we stopped going, I really missed it. I was mad at God at first for taking Dad away, but I know Dad would want us to go.

JOSH: I miss being with my friends at church. I see them at school, but it's not the same. And, Mom, can we start having family devotions again?

JILL: Well . . . all right. We'll see how things go. I'll talk to Grandpa.

GEORGE *(calling from offstage)*: Dinner's ready!

JILL: Dinner? You guys made dinner?

JOSH: Sure did! Wait till you see what we fixed!

JILL: It smells delicious!

(All exit SR.)

Scene 6

*(*JILL *and* GEORGE *enter SL, dressed for church.)*

GEORGE: You're quiet, Jill.

JILL: I'm thinking. It was so good to be in church. I think it's time I get my life back on track.

GEORGE: Good girl.

JILL: The service was beautiful. Everyone seemed so glad to see us. And I feel as though a heaviness has been removed from my heart . . . Oh look, my flowers are beginning to bloom, thanks to your care.

GEORGE: It's good to see a smile in your eyes again.

JILL: Mandy and Josh were both so happy to go back. I guess I didn't realize how much my own anger affected them. Josh even asked if we could start having family devotions again.

George: God is so good, isn't He, Jill? Even when we stumble and fall, He is ready to pick us up and get us going in the right direction again.

JILL: Yes, Dad. I've been through a spiritual winter and now I feel like a new person. I'm glad we celebrate the Lord's resurrection this time of year. For me, spring is a time of renewal, of hope and rejoicing.

GEORGE: I want to thank you again for asking me to live with you and the kids. It means so much to me.

JILL: God planned it. He knew we needed you.

(They exit arm in arm and the lights go down.)

WHO WOULD FOLLOW?

A Short Easter Play

by Dave Tippett

Running Time: Approximately 30-40 minutes

Theme: Following Jesus

Scripture References: Matthew 26:26-30 (NIV); John 17:1-26; 8:3-7 (NIV)

Cast:

NARRATOR—Man or Woman
PETER—Late 20s to early 30s
JESUS—Early 30s (of course)
MATTHEW—Same as Peter
SARAH—Same age range
PHARISEE—Offstage or prerecorded deep male voice

Props:

Fishing net
Simple desk
Scale
Coins
Scrolls
Basket with bread
Cup with wine/juice

Costumes: NARRATOR is dressed in black; all others are dressed for the time period

Production Notes: Simple staging. PETER'S area (fishing) is SR. MATTHEW at a desk CS. Choose music that suits your production. A suggestion for the final song has been provided near the end of the script. Sound effects are available at www.lillenasdrama.com. A follow spot may be used for some of the lighting cues.

(At curtain, music bed for few moments, then light up on NARRATOR *who is standing extreme DSR.)*

NARRATOR: He came to us as no one would suspect. In disguise. As one of us. He went out and took those who would follow . . . truly follow . . . and changed the world. He entered the places where they were, and held out His hand. A hand that assured protection and joy. A hand that promised them that they could be so much more than what they were.

(Light out on NARRATOR; *light up DSR.* PETER, *dressed in working clothes, stands there, net in hands, yelling out to unseen persons.)*

PETER: Stop it! Stop it, I said! What's wrong with you idiots? You nearly rammed my boat! Pay attention! You almost tore my nets too! Stay on your side of the lake! Just wait 'till we make shore and I get my hands on you! To have a night of empty nets and then to have to dodge imbeciles like you! *(Pause)* Yes, you heard me! And I'll repeat it to any man who wants to hear it back on shore! *(Pause)* OK, I'll take on the lot of ya! *(Pause)* Yeah, yeah. Brave words out on the middle of the lake. At least your nets are as empty as mine. Andrew! Wake up! It's time to head in. Hey! What did I say about that tub of yours? You're too close. Turn to port! No! Port, you morons! Stop! We're going to ram! Stop! Stop!

*(*PETER *freezes and his light goes off. Another light comes up DSL.* MATTHEW *is standing, arguing with an unseen person.)*

MATTHEW: Stop! Stop it right now! I will not stand here and be lectured to by a pitiful little . . . pot maker. Taxes are due when taxes are due. Understand? Is that too hard to comprehend? Remember the big guy? Caesar? The one who's gonna expect me to get every little bit of tax you owe? *(Pause)* What? How dare you speak to me like that, you little toad! Maybe time in the Roman stockade will teach you some manners. Hey there . . . come back! You still owe me pot maker! Stop! Thief! Stop! Stop!

(He freezes and his light goes off; NARRATOR *light comes up, with music bed.)*

NARRATOR: He had prepared to come and show them a way out. He wasn't going to use an eloquent sermon. Or brow beat them. Rather, a simple invitation. An invitation to follow, and leave everything they had known. To be with Him. And change the world. The hand extended into their storms. Storms of their own making. Wanting to pull them out. Straining to make contact. A connection. To offer hope and a future.

(Light out on NARRATOR; *light back up on* PETER *who is rolling up his net.)*

PETER: Andrew! The other nets! Don't forget . . . oh, never mind, I'll do it myself! *(Goes a few steps and pretends to roll more nets.* JESUS *approaches from SL and stands in front of* PETER, *who doesn't look up.)* Hey, you want to get off my nets there? Never been on a dock before? *(Looks up)* Who . . . oh, yes, I remember now. Another one of Andrew's friends. Hmpf. Look at you. Aren't you supposed to be some sort of teacher or something? That's what my brother says. Well. Can you fish? Do anything like that? Didn't think so.

JESUS: Peter, go out again into the deep water and let your nets down for the catch.

PETER: Yeah, right. *(JESUS doesn't reply, starts working on the nets again.)* Look, I'm sorry. I've been out all night without catching anything. What makes you think . . . I mean, how do you know that we'll . . . there's simply no fish . . . don't look at me like that! We . . . all right! All right! *(Off to side)* We're going out again! That's what I said! No back talk! I've . . . got this feeling . . .

(Lights fade on PETER and JESUS, lights come up on MATTHEW who is now working at a desk.)

MATTHEW *(grumbling to self)*: No wonder our people get conquered so much. They can't even add and subtract! *(Keeps working as JESUS crosses to desk.)* Yes, can I help You? Here to pay your taxes? Well, you'll have to wait. I'm up to my ears in reports. These Romans want every "T" crossed and every "I" dotted. What's your business here? *(Pause)* Well, don't let the surroundings fool you. It may look like a mess, but I know where everything is and exactly what everyone owes. Sure, these people may not like me much . . . matter of fact, my few friends . . . my only friends . . . are other tax collectors. But hey, I get paid well. Over and under the table, if you know what I mean. *(Pause)* Wait. You aren't with the authorities are you? If you are, I was only kidding about the payments. Really. Uh . . . just what do You want?

JESUS: Matthew. Follow Me.

MATTHEW *(looking around)*: Are you talking to me? What do you mean? Who are you? I . . . oh yes, I recognize you. The fellow that travels about with the fishermen and the like. You . . . uh . . . have a reputation for helping the poor. I'm sure they've told you what I'm like. What I've done to them. I make no apologies. I . . . it's just a living. See all of these things here! *(Starts to gather them up)* Tools for calculating debt. Records and scrolls full of financial information. The scales, the money. These things . . . are all I have. I do my job well. I'm . . . very happy.

JESUS: Follow me.

MATTHEW: Yes, but . . . don't you see? It's all I have. It's important work. Someone has to . . . who will keep track of . . . what will I do . . .

(They stare at each other for a beat, then JESUS *holds out His hands and* MATTHEW *slowly hands over all the things he's been holding.* JESUS *sets them down and holds out His hand.)*

JESUS: Follow Me.

*(*MATTHEW *looks at the things, then takes* JESUS' *hand. After a beat, light goes off on them. Light comes up on* PETER *as he struggles with an obviously heavy net. He hauls it to* JESUS *who has crossed back to him.)*

PETER: This . . . catch. I can't believe it! Never have I seen . . . our boats almost capsized under the load. Every boat brought back hundreds of fish. Fish that weren't there before. How did you know?

JESUS: Peter. Follow Me.

PETER: Huh? What? Me? No, no. You don't know me very well. What I am. What I do. My temper. I fight all the time. Did you know that? Did Andrew tell you about all the rough places I go? What I drink? Thank you for this, *(lifting net)* and thank you for asking. But . . .

JESUS: Follow Me.

PETER: Leave! *(On his knees now)* For I am not worthy. Please go. Take those who are more deserving. *(Shows* JESUS *the net)* I am just a fisherman.

JESUS *(takes net)*: Follow Me. And I will make you fishers of men.

*(*PETER *looks at* JESUS, *then studies his net.)*

JESUS *(holding His hand out)*: Come.

*(*PETER *slowly takes* JESUS' *hand and rises, then light goes off on them. Music up,* NARRATOR *light up. As* NARRATOR *speaks, set is prepared for next scene.)*

NARRATOR: He came, and called, and they responded. Three years together. And now . . . Jerusalem. It was alive with worshipers preparing for Passover. They had entered the city triumphantly, heroes of the people. It was standing room only in the temple. Healings and miracles were happening. They were as strong as they had ever been. They were confident of their mission and more important, confident of their leader. They looked at Him and said to themselves, "We will follow Him anywhere. No matter the cost. No matter the danger. We are here."

Not all the followers felt as strong. Felt as confident. As secure. And a lust for money was about to twist the mind of one of them to the point of betrayal. The crying of a rooster would signal the denial of another that the Master himself had called "The Rock." And on the outskirts of town, two pieces of unfinished wood, fixed together to form a crossbeam, stood waiting for the next victim, casting a long shadow on the walls of the city.

(NARRATOR *light goes off.)*

Song Option

(NARRATOR *light up after song, if one is used.)*

NARRATOR: It was the fifth night after they had entered the city . . .

*(*NARRATOR *light off, stage lights up as the disciples and* JESUS *enter from the back of the sanctuary and approach the set. Traditional Hebrew song(s) of celebration can be used here on sound system.* JESUS *and disciples are talking and joking with each other. They reach the set and take their places, forming small groups.* JESUS *visits each group, greeting His men.)*

JESUS: None of you know how deeply I have longed to eat this Passover meal with you . . . before the time of my suffering begins. I tell you now, I won't partake of it again until I eat and drink it with you in my Father's Kingdom. Serve each other.

(The disciples come forward and take prearranged baskets of bread and cups of juice from JESUS *and proceed to serve the congregation. Stage lights go down here and follow spot comes up to follow singer and* JESUS*. During the serving, soloist comes out and sings a verse and a chorus of a song.* JESUS *then approaches DSC.)*

JESUS: Father . . . the hour has come. Glorify Your Son that the Son may glorify You. I have brought glory to You on earth by completing the work You gave Me to do. And now Father, glorify Me in Your presence with the glory I had with You before the world began. I have told these about You. I pray for them. Father, protect them by the power of Your name . . . the name You gave Me . . . so that they will be united, just as we are. I pray that You not take them out of the world, but to keep them safe from Satan's power. Make them pure and holy. As You have sent Me into the world, I am sending them into the world. For them I sanctify myself, that they may be truly sanctified. My prayer is not for these alone but also for future believers who will come to Me because of their testimony. My prayer for all of them is that they will be of one heart and mind, just as You and I are, Father . . . that just as You are in Me and I am in You, so they will be in us, and the world will believe You sent Me.

(Soloist comes back and finishes song. After soloist is done, follow spot goes off and stage lights come up. JESUS *stands and the disciples approach the stage. Each receives the elements from* JESUS *as they move onto the stage and take their original positions.* JESUS *then walks to DSC; He is carrying a small piece of bread and a container of juice.)*

JESUS *(to the audience, after breaking a piece of bread and holding it up)*: Eat. For this is My body, broken for you. *(Everyone eats.)* Drink. Each one. For this is My blood. It seals the new covenant between God and Man. It is to be poured out for many for the forgiveness of sins. *(All drink.)* And when you gather together, from now on, do this . . . all . . . in remembrance of Me. *(Stage lights dim and soloist comes on. Follow spot comes up on soloist.* JESUS *and disciples exit at same time.)*

Solo Option

(Lights out. Stage lights come up on a woman, SARAH, *as she comes out to CS. She is dressed in period costume.)*

SARAH *(looking around)*: This . . . is the way He came. I recognize the street. It's so quiet now. But then. The noise. The screaming. The shouting. And there He was. Having to carry that cross by himself. If I could have gotten through to help I would have. You see, I am a follower of His too. Because of what He did for me. For how He reached into my life. And gave me hope and a new start. How He called me. I can still remember the day . . .

(Stage lights dim. SARAH *turns her back to the audience, staying perfectly still. Dissonant music comes up, angry crowd SFX.* SARAH *turns around to continue. Follow spot is on her. She looks around wildly, as if cornered.)*

SARAH: Oh no, they've found me again! *(Runs back and forth across stage)* I thought I lost them! *(Pointing in the back)* There! Oh, no! There they are! They're picking up rocks . . . stones . . . No! No! Please! Wait! I won't do it again! Please! Give me another chance! Don't! Please!

(She falls and curls up in a ball as mob SFX intensifies. Then a shadow falls on the prone figure of the woman. It is JESUS *who is walking up the center aisle, interrupting the path of light from the follow spot. On the sound track, the mob noises cut back some,* PHARISEE *starts.)*

PHARISEE *(offstage or prerecorded)*: Rabbi. It's so good to see You again. And You're just in time to help us with a problem. *(*JESUS *reaches the platform, and sits down on the edge.)* It's quite a dilemma. You see, this . . . woman . . . has been caught in adultery. The very act. Now, the law commands that we stone such women. What . . . do You say? (JESUS *continues to look down, writing on ground with a stick.)* Surely, Rabbi, You must see the only course open to us by the law? Please, share with us how You would resolve . . . such a matter. Hmmmm?

(Mob SFX die out quickly as all have stopped speaking to hear what JESUS *is going to say.* JESUS *stands and looks directly into the follow spot.)*

JESUS: He who is without sin . . . let him cast the first stone. *(Beat, then to* SARAH*)* Is there no one left to condemn you?

SARAH *(looking around)*: None . . . none, Lord. No one.

JESUS: Neither do I condemn you. Go . . . and sin no more.

*(*JESUS *holds out His hand to her. She looks up, not sure whether to take His hand or not . . . then slowly takes it. He helps her up, then exits.* SARAH *stands there looking after Him. She lowers her head and freezes. Follow spot goes out, stage lights come up, and* SARAH *address the audience again.)*

SARAH: He knew the kind of person I was. And yet, He showed mercy. Compassion. He offered me a way out. A way out of a lifestyle that I was drowning in. Simply by reaching out His hand. And I've followed Him ever since. I saw His miracles. The healings. Followed Him here. To the city. Saw Him on this road. Saw Him . . . on the tree. And heard of His rising. An empty tomb! I'm going there now, to see for myself. I have no doubts, though. He is alive. Today. Now. For the hand that took mine that fateful day . . . the hand that stopped the stones from flying, and gave me a new chance . . . that hand that was pierced for all of us . . . is now holding the hand of God. And with His other hand, He reaches out, longing to hold us. Close. Tight. Forever.

(She exits, as music comes up, stage lights dim.)

Solo Option

(A soloist may come out and conclude program. Recommend soloist sings a song related to the resurrection such as "He's Alive" by Don Francisco, or "Arise, My Love." If you choose to take this option, have all the disciples [less one, which represents Judas' absence] come out during the song and take their original places. Their mood should be very solemn. At the height of the chorus, have JESUS *come down the center aisle, and have one or two of the men see Him and actually run to Him. Then have the rest come to Him as He comes onto the stage, with a final grouping of all the men sitting around Him as music concludes and lights go out. You might also consider having the minister/pastor come out and give a short message or concluding thought.)*